This book belongs to

____

Given with love by

____

Our Mother Too

Mary Embraces the World

Shannon K. Evans and
Eric A. Clayton

ILLUSTRATED BY
Ryan McQuade

Paulist Press
New York / Mahwah, NJ

Cover illustration by Ryan McQuade
Cover and book design by Lynn Else

Library of Congress Control Number: 2024945702

ISBN 978-0-8091-5755-6 (hardcover)
ISBN 978-0-8091-8922-9 (e-book)

Published by Paulist Press
997 Macarthur Boulevard
Mahwah, NJ 07430
www.paulistpress.com

Printed and bound in the
United States of America

by Versa Press, Inc.
East Peoria, IL
February 2025

For Alyosha, Moses, Taavi, Oscar, and Thea

For Elianna and Camira

The angel arrived unannounced and unexpectedly. Mary had never seen such a thing.

"God is with you," the angel said. "Do not be afraid."

But Mary was not afraid. Mary was curious.

How had this angel entered her room? It had not come through a door or a window.

"You will have a baby," the angel said.

And then Mary felt something new stir inside of her. It felt like love. It felt like delight.

I want everyone to feel like this, she thought. And the angel left her.

Mary's baby grew.

From a baby to a boy. From a boy to a teenager. From a teenager to a man.

As Jesus grew, Mary's love for him did too.

She laughed as he played. She encouraged him as he made friends. She danced with him at weddings. Her love followed him when he grew up and left home.

And when he gave his life, Mary's heart broke.

"Who can I share my love and delight with now?" she wondered.

Then, three days after his death, Jesus came back. He arrived in Mary's little room, unannounced and unexpectedly.

"Hi, Mom," he said. "Do not be afraid."

But Mary was not afraid. She was full of joy.

And she was curious. "How can this be?" she asked.

"Not even death can stop God's love and delight," her son replied.

"Not death, not doors, not windows," Mary smiled. She kept the thought tucked deep in her heart.

Mary was excited to tell others about this good news. And she wasn't the only one—Jesus's friends were, too. They strapped on their sandals and picked up their walking sticks and went far and wide to share what they had learned about hope and mercy from Jesus.

But it wasn't always easy. Jesus's friends often felt discouraged. Mary knew she could help. And so, again and again, the Holy Spirit led her to visit Jesus's friends right when they needed comfort and support the most.

Eventually, the Spirit brought her far from familiar places and into foreign lands.

"Do not be afraid," she said kindly. But the people were. She could see it in their eyes. And her words didn't seem to help because the people didn't understand them.

What could she do? The Holy Spirit never failed.

And then, just like that, she saw her son. With him were angels, singing and carrying a crown.

"Hi, Mom," Jesus said. "Time to come home." He winked. "I have a plan."

"But my work here isn't done," Mary said. "You saw the pain on their faces. These people need to feel God's love and delight too. I can help them."

"You're right," Jesus said. "And you will. You just have to speak their language."

Mary remembered that when the Holy Spirit had first come upon their friends, they had all started speaking in new languages.

"You're right," Mary said. "But for them to feel safe with me, I need to look like them. I want to be their mother too."

And Jesus smiled. Because that's what he had wanted all along. So, he took his mom's hand and led her to heaven to get ready.

Mary wanted each person to know that God lived in them—that God was in all places, all people. She wanted them to know that God lived in their culture, in their homes, and in their neighbors.

And so, Mary set out to travel the world. Death couldn't stop her and neither could doors nor windows.

Mary went to India and multiplied buttermilk to show kindness.

Our Lady of Good Health

Mary went to El Salvador and changed the flow of lava.

Our Lady of Peace

Mary went to Mexico and turned fear into flowers.

Our Lady of Guadalupe

Mary went to Vietnam,
and rainforest leaves
became medicine.

Our Lady of La Vang

Mary went to France
and healed sickness
with water.

Our Lady of Lourdes

Mary went to Portugal, and even the sun said a prayer.

Our Lady of Fátima

Mary went to Japan, and
suddenly deaf ears could hear.

Our Lady of Akita

Mary went to Rwanda, and years later, hope grew from sadness.

Our Lady of Kibeho

Although she dressed in different clothing and appeared in different ways, Mary was still the same person every time: a woman and a mother who wanted every person to experience God's love.

Mary comes to you too—wherever you are, wherever you live. Looking like you. Wearing the same kind of clothes as you.

Mary says to you, "Do not be afraid. Instead, be kind. Be brave. Be curious. God is with you."

She wants you to find God in your friends and family, in the birdsong and the tall trees, in your prayers, in neighbors, and in strangers.

Mary hopes you will talk to her son. She's Jesus's mother, after all. And so, she's your mother too.

Most of all, she wants you to know that no matter who you are, no matter where you live, no matter what you look like, you are loved. And God delights in you.

AUTHORS

Shannon K. Evans is the author of *The Mystics Would Like a Word*, *Feminist Prayers for My Daughter*, and *Rewilding Motherhood*. Shannon loves Mary in all her forms but has a special place in her heart for Our Lady of Guadalupe. She and her family make their home in central Iowa.

Eric A. Clayton is the author of *My Life with the Jedi: The Spirituality of Star Wars* and *Cannonball Moments: Telling Your Story, Deepening Your Faith*. Eric loves to tell the story of Our Lady of Aranzazu and thinks her sanctuary in Spain might be the holiest place in Europe. He lives in Maryland with his wife and two daughters.

ILLUSTRATOR

Ryan McQuade is an illustrator and graphic designer from Nashville, Tennessee. For the past decade, he has worked in editorial design, creating book covers and illustrations for magazines and online publications. A lover of the spiritual, Ryan uses his art to explore the often unasked questions in life and to bring fresh perspective to our deeply held beliefs.

The Hail Mary

Hail, Mary, full of grace,
the Lord is with thee.
Blessed art thou amongst women
and blessed is the fruit of thy womb, Jesus.
Holy Mary, Mother of God,
pray for us sinners,
now and at the hour of our death.
Amen.

My Mother Too

Holy Mary, Jesus's mother,
And my mother too,
Help me to be kind and loving,
Strong and brave like you.

Help me see in all God's children
Jesus Christ your loving Son
Show me how to talk to Jesus
And have love for everyone.
Amen.